Let's Wonder About Science

ELEMENTS, COMPOUNDS AND MIXTURES

J.M. Patten, Ed.D.

The Rourke Book Co., Inc.
Vero Beach, Florida 32964

PHOTO CREDITS
All photos © J.M. Patten

Library of Congress Cataloging-in-Publication Data

Patten, J.M., 1944-
    Elements, compounds and mixtures / J.M. Patten.
    p. cm.
    Includes index.
    ISBN 1-55916-127-2
    1. Chemistry—Juvenile literature. [1. Chemistry.] I. Title. II. Series:
Patten, J.M., 1944-   Let's wonder about science.
QD35.P27   1995
540—dc20   95-4203
                                                         CIP
                                                          AC

Printed in the USA

TABLE OF CONTENTS

WHAT IS SCIENCE?

The story of **elements, compounds** and **mixtures** puts real science right in your hands. It's really interesting and fun to know about.

You will find out about gold and silver, how salt and sugar are made in nature, and that many things can be mixed together. The scientist in you must already be wondering, "Is this about money, food and soda pop?"

Let's read all about elements, compounds and mixtures and find out.

Children make great scientists because they ask so many questions.

ELEMENTS COME FIRST

Matter is any living or nonliving thing that takes up space. Now, that's just about everything!

Scientists know of about 100 different kinds of atoms, or tiny ingredients, that nature can use to make all the matter in the world.

Things made of only one kind of matter, like iron, mercury, copper, silver and gold, are called elements.

Helium is an element because it's made of only one kind of matter—helium atoms. The helium in these balloons makes them rise.

Another name for these little "building blocks" of matter is elements.

Some elements you might already know are oxygen, helium, copper, iron, silver and gold. There are many more and some have very long, fancy names.

THE PERIODIC TABLE

Scientists have made a chart called the **periodic table** that lists all the known elements. This chart makes elements easier to learn about.

Elements join together, or **bond,** to make matter—trees, mountains, cars, french fries, pizzas, CDs, water, air, chairs, people—almost everything.

Some things are made from one element, like gold. Most matter is made from more than one kind of element. Scientists can use the periodic table to see how elements can join together to make different kinds of matter.

Many different elements join together in special ways to make all living and nonliving things— like you and this tiger cat.

ELEMENTS TO COMPOUNDS

Do you want to see some science magic? Elements can join together to make something brand new—and so different, you can't even see what you started with!

When elements bond, a compound appears. Compounds look, feel and behave differently from the elements that make them.

Do you shake salt on your french fries? Salt is a compound made from two different elements. One element in salt is sodium, a silvery metal. The other is chlorine, a poisonous, smelly green gas. It's hard to believe that when they join together, good old table salt is made.

Elements that bond together are called compounds, like water, sugar and salt.

WE STAY TOGETHER— COMPOUNDS

Compounds stay together. They don't come apart by themselves. The salt on your french fries cannot turn back into sodium and chlorine on its own. The bonds that hold compounds together are very strong.

Two elements—sodium and chlorine—bond together to make the salt on popcorn.

Is this sugar or salt? Both compounds look almost alike but—wow—do they taste different!

Compounds are all around us. Some, like salt, contain only two elements. Others contain many more. Sugar is a compound made from three elements—carbon, hydrogen and oxygen. Salt may look like sugar, but it sure doesn't taste like sugar. That's because salt and sugar are made from different elements.

It's important to remember that a compound must have at least two elements.

WE COME APART—MIXTURES

Mixtures are a combination of parts that can be easily separated, or taken apart. The parts in mixtures don't bond together. This makes them very different from compounds.

Do you build sand castles at the seashore? If you take a close look, you can see that beach sand is a mixture. You'll see sand, of course, but you might also find pieces of rocks and sea shells, bits of seaweed and maybe even a tiny crab—all mixed together.

If you are careful and go slowly, you can separate each part. You might use a sifter to separate big and little parts.

Isn't this fun? Mixtures can be taken apart. Compounds are bonded together.

If you search or sift through sand, you can find it's many parts—bits of rock and stone, shell and seaweed.

STIR US UP—SOLUTIONS

Solutions are a special kind of mixture. In a solution, all the parts become evenly mixed. Let's mix up a drink and find out about them.

First, choose a good flavor—maybe cherry—and pour the powder into a pitcher. Next we add cold water and take a quick look. The drink looks darker red at the bottom of the pitcher where the powder is sitting.

Now we'll take a big spoon and stir carefully. Let's look again. The drink in every part of the pitcher is now the same shade of red. Let's wonder what happened.

The powder and water mixed together evenly to form a solution. This is called **dissolving.** The drink will taste sweet all the way through. Let's drink up!

This pizza is a mixture of crust, sauce, cheese and meats.

MORE ABOUT SOLUTIONS

Water is good for dissolving and making solutions. You can make good things to eat and drink with water—like gelatin and iced tea. Other solutions made with water are pretty handy.

Soda pop, tea, milk and muddy puddles are all solutions—liquid kinds of mixtures.

Be careful—most cleaning solutions are poisonous and should not be tasted.

Soap dissolves in water. Now, that's good for washing clothes and dirty faces—or even blowing bubbles.

Turpentine is another good dissolver. Paint dissolves in turpentine like drink mix dissolves in water. Turpentine is good for cleaning paint brushes and paint-covered fingers. It is also poisonous!

ELEMENTS, COMPOUNDS AND MIXTURES

Let's think about the things you found out. That's how you learn and remember.

Matter is any living or nonliving thing that takes up space. All kinds of matter are made from about 100 different elements. These elements are listed on the periodic table.

Compounds, like sugar and salt, are made from at least two different elements that bond together. Compounds do not come apart by themselves.

Mixtures are a combination of parts that can be easily separated. The parts in mixtures don't bond together.

Solutions are special mixtures made with liquids, like drink mixes or salt water. The parts become dissolved, spreading out evenly all the way through the liquid.

Soap and water mix together to make soap suds to wash the dust and road grime off this sports car.

GLOSSARY

bond (BAHND) — when two or more elements join together to form a compound

compound (KOM pownd) — a substance made up of two or more elements bonded together to make something new

dissolve (dih ZAHLV) — mixing a liquid with something else to form a solution

element (EL uh ment) — atoms, or tiny parts, that make up all the different kinds of matter in the world

matter (MAT er) — all living and nonliving things that take up space

mixture (MIKS chur) — a combination of parts that can be easily separated

periodic table (peer ee AH dik TAY buhl) — the chart, or list, of all the elements

solution (suh LOO shun) — a mixture made with water or some other liquid

Water is a compound and can't be taken apart. The old stump is a mixture and will rot away, breaking down into the parts it is made of.

INDEX